THE POWER OF
ADVERSITY

THE SETBACKS OF LIFE ARE ONLY SETUPS FOR
EXTRAORDINAIRE COMEBACKS

BYRON WESLEY

TABLE OF CONTENTS

Preface III
Overview VII
Synopsis IX
Acknowledgement XI
Self-Declaration XIII

PART I

1. In the Beginning 17
2. Guardian Angel 23
3. The Wait 27
4. Home Sweet Home 35

PART II

5. Choice 43
The life-altering interview 50
Mindset of Choice 53
6. The Transformation 55
I just want to be happy (Interview)
59 Transformational Moments 64
Media Giant 67
Past, Present & Future 73
Optimizing "Transformational Moments"
78 **7. My Journey is my Journey 81**
The Strongest Tree 85
I felt like an outdated toy (Interview) 89
III Dynamic E's 94

CONTINUED

PART III

8. Reinvent Yourself 105
Back Against the Ropes 108
Forgive 112
Happiness 120
Habits 128
Anchor or Engine 132
Keystone Conclusion 138

PREFACE

The birth of a baby for many is extremely magical, heart warming, and simply unforgettable; one of life's most cherished moments. Stressful and exhausting yes, but the emotional satisfaction outweighs it all. Some would even proclaim that very few experiences in life compare. Unfortunately, this isn't the case for all children that are delivered into this world. Over 1,000,000 children annually are delivered, examined, and handed off for further adoption processing "adoption processing". Get where I'm headed with a book titled ***"The Power of Adversity"***? To the majority open arms, family members, loving hearts, and enriching environments are ubiquitous. While for the remaining percentage it is only a figment of the imagination. The type of imagination that if left unaddressed, seems to linger and foster emotions of inferiority, guilt, and abandonment. What exactly is it like to be adopted? A question that I'm far too familiar with! Occasionally it is followed by, do you know your biological parents, or why did they even give you up? Being an adoptee, these questions hit close to home, as I know the challenges first hand and wanted to share my journey, obstacles, and triumphs. Like how an unwanted infant given up at birth with no family, and what seemed like a unpromising future, remained optimistic despite adversity. Being matched at just a couple of months old to a small town country raised woman, not only inspired me to pay it forward, but to immerse myself in the understanding of human cognition and behavior. Curiosity led me to the doorsteps of a prodigious university in South Florida to study Neurobiology, Neuroscience, Human Cognition and Behavior. Interviews with over 200 adoptees narrowed my focus to addressing the most common psychological deficits. Whether adopted or not, this journey was intended to inspire self-actualization and promote self-discovery one reader at a time, no matter the origin.

Furthermore, I will encourage you to share quotes and content that impacts you onto your social networks and within your social groups. Join me in my goal to inspire and encourage those in which we come into contact with.

FOLLOW US

@ThePowerofAdversity
#ThePowerofAdversity

OVERVIEW

This eBook edition of **"The Power of Adversity"** is one the most powerful, heart clenching, and transformational depictions written to date. This two part self-examining composition is intended to elicit and invigorate all walks of life. Explicitly illustrating the gut-wrenching journey of being adopted and the affects of being given up for adoption immediately following birth. Despite being born into adversity, motherless, and unwanted, I refused to allow circumstances to dictate life's outcome. I discuss my youthful rebellion as well my successful transformations throughout my lifespan. Using disadvantages as motivation, I lunged toward my desired future; inspiring each individual I cross paths with. Proclaiming that with an optimistic outlook, positive self-image, and a determined mind-set, anyone can tackle life's challenges, as they inevitably reveal themselves. Readers will discover the necessary components to reaching total self-confidence and self-actualization while alleviating adverse psychological deficits.

VIII

This eBook is packed with inspiring stories that will appeal to all adoptive parents, their children, family members, and friends alike. By conducting over 200 interviews with adoptees, I was able to decipher and provide diverse perspectives from all demographics. This story exemplifies that resilience and triumph lie at the end of every obstacle in life.

SYNOPSIS

This eBook edition of **"The Power of Adversity"** is one the most powerful, heart clenching and transformational depictions written to date. This two-part self-examining composition is intended to elicit and invigorate all walks of life.

> **"**
> I want the world to know my story and understand that our past doesn't dictate our present nor our future...
> **"**
>
> BYRON WESLEY

ACKNOWLEDGMENT

When we met my life began, I admit, my life prior to us meeting wasn't pleasant. It wasn't the life any infant should endure. Given up, unwanted, and adopted, I accepted it. Nonetheless, it planted seeds of resiliency. Our paths fused so aesthetically. You watered, you nurtured, and you provided the proper amount of sunshine. I grew, I loved, I rebelled, I listened, and I developed, into the gentleman that stands before you today, as I proclaim this to you. Your tears, my tears, our tears are symbolic to our imperfectly perfect journey. This particular journey, this life, this outcome wouldn't be possible, if one facet was altered. You acted as my numbing agent, my eraser, and my holistic healer. Yes, Katie Gillings you are my rock, my stone, and my world. Using only language to describe your impact is a disservice and insufficient. You are my mom, my dad, my family, my one and only mother. I've come to the realization mom, you don't have to carry nine months or experience labor to be a mother.

Also, have I mentioned how courageous I find your actions to be; a single mother taking on "Life" literally and with grace! You are the epitome of a hero and I want the universe to know "I love you"

So with that, I dedicate this book to you.

ACKNOWLEDGMENT

SELF-DECLARATION

I .... [Insert Name Here]

Declare that my mental health, happiness and overall well-being are a priority. I am fully invested in identifying exactly what areas of life need adjustments. Once identified, I will enter into a never ending rhythm of self-growth. I will utilize this book and the tools provided as a guide to fine-tune my innate greatness! No longer will I create nor accept excuses for any self-sabotaging behaviors. Past circumstance doesn't define me. I acknowledge that in order to successfully design my future, I must take deliberate action in the present. My future is illustrious and my opportunities are limitless. Knowing this, fuels my drive to propel me forward in the most enriching manner possible. Yes, I am fully aware that the road ahead will come with it's share of difficulties! Mentally, physically and spiritually I am up for the challenge. I understand that I maybe criticized, mocked and misunderstood by family members, friends and or strangers, yet I am completely OK with that. This is my journey and I'm ready to personalize it into the most amazing experience possible!

Sign:................ **Date:**............

SELF-DECLARATION

PART I

CHAPTER 1
IN THE BEGINNING

"THERE ARE NO UNWANTED CHILDREN. JUST UNFOUND FAMILIES"
-NATIONAL ADOPTION CENTER

On the 3rd of February in 1985 at 0902 hours, a chocolate chip infant was delivered in a California NICU, but not without some level of uneasiness. Imagine with me if you will, a 7lb 2 ounces newborn, with a head full of curly hair, beady eyes, absolutely no sound, just fixated stares of suspicion towards this new and unfamiliar environment. Fluorescent lights, voices, faces, smells, sounds, and physical contact; talk about a complete sensory overload. Panic quickly set in for the medical staff attending the delivery. When the transition from womb to physician's arms didn't initiate the glass-shattering outcry as expected. Was this the beginning of a life filled with possible medical complications or a highly unusual journey to resilience? This spontaneous cry is a milestone, an indicator in which the medical staff looks for.

Signaling that the child has begun clearing amniotic fluids from it's lungs and has adequate respiration. The unwillingness to cry perpetuated concern with frightening thoughts of a not so positive outcome. The first 1 to 5 minutes was spent being evaluated and thoroughly examined. They conducted the required APGAR testing, which focuses on five indications of good physical health. As my little beady eyes continued to jump from object to object throughout the room, the apprehensive team focused their efforts diligently on my breathing. The thing was, I was breathing normal the entire time, all they needed was a cry, but for whatever reason I just wouldn't produce it. Scoring a 1 for respiratory effort, out of a possible 0,1, or 2, the team concluded that even with having an abnormal experience, my heart rate and breathing were given proper approval. The team then transitioned to monitoring muscle tone, reflexes, and skin color. With one glimmer or an ounce of outcry my APGAR testing would've resulted in a rare, but perfect 10 out of 10.

So, during what's considered a traditional birth, I should've been delivered, suctioned with a bulb syringe, produced a cry and wiped free of the amniotic fluids that covered my body. Instinctively, one may think. Following that sequence of events, I should've been placed chest to chest with my biological mother. This is where the absorption of her body heat could've taken place. There is power in a mother's warmth. Her warmth alone would instigate the production of chemicals in my brain to initiate growth. That short period of time spent in the arms of my biological mother, would stimulate the deep emotional and physical connections needed, to establish the foundation of our everlasting relationship. According to what actually transpired during that sensitive period, makes that sound like an improbable fairy-tale. But, here it was; life's first lesson. Something's just aren't fair. My delivery happened to be a little dissimilar from "tradition" deliveries, you've either heard about or experienced. My biological mother wasn't elated and it wasn't due to labor exhaustion; there was neither excitement nor celebration to my arrival into this world.

Picture a birth where the baby isn't hugged, held or touched by it's mother; where no smiles, tears or joy are present. Just repetitive attempts to dislodge this infant from her womb and a destitute of love, affection and emotion. That mother's warmth I mentioned earlier, substituted by artificial warming lights, this replaced the natural method of warmth produced by skin-to-skin contact. The upside is that the lights visually assisted the physician in properly facilitating the delivery. The secondary rush of oxytocin was omitted, which is often initiated by a mother's soft touch or her distinctive scent. Oxytocin is widely referred to as the cuddle

IN THE BEGINNING

hormone, associated with long lasting bonding and trust. The newborn habituates to the unique imprinted smell of its mother, which would normally induce calmness, pain reduction and a desire for further contact; No bonding present here. Usually, this period is spent with heightened levels of incitation, capturing of pictures and tons of celebrating for such a joyous and indelible moment. Yet again, this aspect of my introduction was quite dissimilar. A nurse on staff performed the cutting of my umbilical cord, then being placed inside the incubator and wheeled off.

In conventional circumstances, the father, a designated family member or friend of the family performs this unforgettable moment. With that being the last time I would be in close proximity to her, the ability to locate her imprinted smell would go to waste. The name, location and existence of my biological parents till this day remain an enigma. This 44 by 53 in incubator located in the NICU, would now be considered my home. Scheduled rounds made by the nurses on shift, became a source of human interaction and affection. Some days better than others, according to RN Jennifer E. Between shifts, time would be spent playing with toes, sleeping, eating, gazing and of course biological functions. Hmm, Sounds like the typical life of an infant, minus one essential element, a "mother" or a family desperately waiting my discharge to take me home. This, "this" transitional phase could only be described as dismal, bleak and filled with confusion, as if processing this new environment wasn't enough.

Only Days after being born and here I am already being placed in baby isolation. If you had to make an educated guess as to what my future would manifest into, I'm sure initial thoughts of happiness, prosperity and abundance, wouldn't make the list. Parent after parent, family member after family member (Click Click Click) Photos, videos, laughter and sounds of rejoicing cries from other families would flood the room periodically, which would soon be followed by complete silence. (Machine beeps)

CHAPTER 2
THE GUARDIAN ANGEL

A few moments following my anomalous delivery signified the beginning of my transitional phase. From birth to the commencement of paperwork and the in-processing

"CERTAIN PEOPLE CROSS YOUR LIFE AS GUARDIAN ANGELS & SOME CONNECTIONS CAN'T BE EXPLAINED OFF WORDS ALONE" -UNKNOWN

stages of my adoption, hmmm I'd rather just call it "My Journey". While a dozen or so families wrapped up their final examinations, mine was just getting underway. Families asking their nurses, last minute questions in their mandatory parental classes. Nurses were reiterating information to the families; to assuage the overt nervousness and to reinsure they had the proper information. These courses were specifically designed to prepare couples for precautionary measures as they embark on this parental journey. Lastly, families would sign documents with their corresponding doctors, in order to be discharged home, to enjoy their precious addition(s) to the family.

Here I am at just a few minutes old and already being placed on the agencies adoption list, talk about being dispensable and unwanted. Entirely oblivious to the swift and drastic changes approaching, that would forever alter my life's trajectory. Some thousand's of miles away in the beautiful sunshine state of Florida. A highly influential and respected entrepreneur by the name of "Katie Gillings" would begin the immense adoption process. These detailed and strenuous evaluations, would comb through her finances, screen her psychologically and evaluate her living conditions. Adoption agencies implement these rigorous stipulations and requirements in order to protect us adoptees from ending up in the hands of just any individual, family or foreseen danger. Katie underwent this meticulous, tedious and laborious process with a vision and guidance from God.

Directors have been quoted saying, "this journey isn't cut out for the weak-hearted" or "everybody here won't be approved." Resonating messages like these discourage and stain the minds of waiting adopting families. These blunt but veracious statements or grueling evaluations couldn't detour Katie from her vision of adopting. Her training in motherhood began rather early in life. Being raised in a small town, on the outskirts of Central Florida is where it would all begin. At the time, Ocala Florida was densely populated with racial tension and community division. This wasn't enough to stop the household from sticking together and showering one another with unconditional love. Growing up with 12 siblings and being among the oldest Its no secret where her loving and nurturing ways stem from. Precocious abilities were developed quickly through taking on big sister responsibilities at such a young age. This was mentally preparing Katie for the largest job and responsibility of her life; "Motherhood." Ever since a young girl, Katie would envision the type of life she wanted to live. Always dreaming of providing service and empowerment to women of all walks of life. Not finding ideal opportunities in Ocala, lead to her running away.

THE GUARDIAN ANGEL

You would think she'd be crippled by fear and just the thought alone, but no. Her high school graduation couldn't come quick enough to execute her plans. Ending up in Miami, Florida with family is where she would continue to design life on her terms. Starting with a job as construction surveyor, measuring and examining construction work. Working there would only increase her desire to risk it all and start her business. So building her cosmetics business was where her passion would illuminate. No experience, just a vision and the belief in her capabilities. The thriving business was born and named "Katie's Cosmetics." Life was blossoming and beginning to take shape. She would go onto purchase a beautiful two-bedroom house that was fenced, fully furnished, but yet still empty. There was one major component missing to complete her dream life.

CHAPTER 3
THE WAIT

> "HAVE THE PATIENCE TO WAIT FOR THE RIGHT MOMENT AND THE COURAGE TO ACCEPT THAT YOU'VE WAITED FOR NOTHING" -UNKNOWN

So finally, with the completion of numerous interviews, financial screenings, surprise home visits and rigorous paperwork, begins the dreadful waiting period for that highly anticipated "phone call". This isn't just your typical phone call, this "phone call" from the social worker at the Catholic Adoption Agency, is everything and will inform Katie that a possible match has been made. What exactly is a "Match"? Basically with the information provided and discussed between the adopter(s) and adoptive agencies, a suitable adopter(s) and the right child based on the needs of each party will be placed together. But, of course, the phone call isn't instantly received without some form of delay or impedance, so Katie's wait continues. Imagine being extremely high on alert; for something in particular. As in this case the "phone call", but instead everything else aside from what you're actually looking for seems to flow directly towards you. It's as if seconds turn into hours, hours into months, months into years and years into eternity.

Time continues to creep pass and there is absolutely no "phone call" pertaining to a possible match or yet any progression in the placement progress. Meanwhile, as the anticipation grew, Katie decided to road trip up the east coast with the destination being Cleveland, Ohio to visit family. This trip was planned with the hopes of being distracted from agonizing thoughts of when and how the "phone call" would actually transpire. Stopping every couple of hundred miles to not only stretch but to call the agency and check on the status for updates. I'm sure the repetitive calling can easily be mistaken as bothersome or even a bit abrasive, but I'd like to view it as determination; Ensuring the completion of a set objective.

Arriving in Cleveland after a supposedly therapeutic commute, lead to increased levels of anxiety, which triggered thoughts of "what if I don't get matched". This fluctuating emotional rollercoaster could only be alleviated by one source. That source being the phone call from the agency divulging that a possible match is officially in the works. The next couple of days for Katie happen to be the hardest, not even the amusement and entertainment of loved ones could keep her concentration at bay and off what she so desperately desired. Every time the phone would ring, I could only imagine it sending any expecting adoptive parent into a set of spiraling thoughts starting with "what am I actually going to say" or "what if I am not suitable". The family congregated in the kitchen around the table top; as the room continued to increasingly fill with laughter and joy. Just what the doctor would recommend, for a person experiencing such a perplex and mentally taxing situation; Family time and an abundance of laughter. Ahh Nostalgia set in, as memory lane was embarked upon; stories of early day childhood to present day experiences were poked fun at and laughed over.

Finally, in the distance a telephone rung, promptly silencing the kitchen; could this be it? The very thought that I'm sure raced through the minds of those present. With expectancy levels already approaching maximum threshold, this is just what the family needed, another false alarm. Mid-evening of her fifth day in Cleveland here it was; possibly the phone call she had been expecting. Reluctantly, she makes here way over to the phone as it continues to ring; she pauses and just stands there. Overcome with hesitation. All the built up anticipation, left her physically paralyzed and unable to register anything else at that current moment. After mustering up and gaining composure she sits, and then answers the ringing phone, the first word to escape her mouth was a subtle "Hello". The family filters in, surrounding her as she partakes in possibly the most impactful phone call of her life. The agency's representative returns the greetings and begins to cover the specifics of the possible match, she led with the gender and the name, and Katie couldn't do anything, but listen. The agent even mentioned that I had already been assigned a name. "DAVID" David is what they called me, it wasn't officially documented, but it's what they called me around the Catholic Adoption Agency and foster home. So I'm guessing I was given a temporary nickname for six months. Still remaining silent, Katie processed all of the incoming information, although she specifically expressed her desire to adopt an infant girl. With the gender news in opposition, I would guess the breathtaking excitement outweighed the discontent. Did I mention that her vision from god revealed a different scenario, which involved a baby boy being born and delivered into the world? Remaining optimistic as the agent continued revealing specifics, details such as age and race. Suddenly, like a river after a downpour Katie's questions discharged so effortlessly, which in return were politely followed by answers from the agencies representative. Katie scheduled for the first available appointment, to come in and complete the remaining steps of the matching process. This is where I would be on placed in the company of the adopter to see if we "match". Hmm, If not, well, then I go back to the foster home and the process resets and starts all over again. But, if I were actually "matched", this would possibly be the last time I'm exchanged into the hands of yet another unfamiliar face. Lets see how this goes. So as the call neared it's ending, the last statement made was, Katie reconfirming that she will head out tonight. She hangs up and just stares at the phone with her hand still affixed, she stood quiet as a tear ran down her face and fell onto the backside of her hand. She looked up in the direction of where the family was gathered and mumbled, "I have a baby boy" "I have a baby boy" "I'm going to be a mother" crying tears of happiness, relief and contentment. The "wait" and emotional rollercoaster could possibly be coming to an end. Immediately, she started packing to return home, cutting the trip short in order to begin her newfound journey to mother hood.

CHAPTER 4
HOME SWEET HOME

This morning had a peculiar beginning; Rather than the normal routine of me waking up on my own, in the wee hours. My foster parents, switching on this old indelible ceiling fan, interrupted my sleep.

> "ADOPTING MEANS OPENING YOUR HOME, AND HEART TO A LIFE YOU'VE NEVER KNOWN"
> -MICHAEL GOVE

That ceiling fan produced such immense radiating light, which happen to be positioned directly above my crib, so you can only imagine the intensity of the light. It swayed back and forth making this distinct noise that held my attention, as if I knew it could fall at any moment. As my eyes opened and acclimated to the uncomfortable brightness, my foster's had already began to clothe me; for what? I wasn't sure! I was a baby, all I wanted to do was sleep. My wee hour wakeup routines were invariably accompanied with distress calls, signaling feed me, feed me. You know the relentless and notorious suckle sounding cries; that a hungry and agitated infant exhibits. Yea, that was me basically every morning until my what seemed like insatiable formula hunger, was satisfied, according to my foster's.

This particular morning was different as I mentioned before, still in trance from the abrupt wake up, noise and bright lights. I calmly cooperated while my court assigned fosters continued to prepare me for whatever it was that was next. My face stained with curiosity, but not sure if it was directed towards the ceiling fan or as to, "why" the change in routine? Next I'm being buckled into the car seat followed by the sounds of the car doors closing. Arriving at the Catholic Adoption Agency where I'm usually with my foster's and agency representatives in a waiting room. There was an influx in the amount of disturbance that I was accustomed to, as unfamiliar faces circulated in, out and around the examination room. Physical contact was at an all time high, so being unaccustomed to it all, slightly made the experience disturbing and unsettling. So I reacted the best way I knew how with an intense ear-shattering cry, which seemed to go in my favor in previous attempts, so I gave it a shot. But, this attempt was unsuccessful as countless unfamiliar faces continued to pick me up, place me back down, place cold metal objects against my upper chest and lower back, probing objects in my ear and every other orifice.

Unaware that these unfamiliar faces were social workers, nurses and pediatricians conducting an examination for "Out Processing" purposes. I unknowingly associated the examination with annoyance and pestering, just as my unrelenting cry suggested. As the routine examination came to a completion the room gradually started to reduce in traffic and sound disturbance. Eventually met with silence, and then followed the incremental beeps from the monitoring machines placed throughout the room. This very distinctive set of hard bottom shoes echoed loudly throughout the hallway, easing closer and closer as if they were headed directly towards me, but they ceased abruptly. Suddenly an overshadowing silhouette appeared, that seemed to extend its reach toward me; it picked me up and placed me in its warm crevice. As we began to move (Click Click Click). The hard bottomed shoes made contact with the concrete floor. The distinctive echo resumed, but this time with me in tote. My longest experience out of the 44 by 53 in crib was short lived, which ended in a well-illuminated, yet dinky office. There was this energy of uncontainable excitement also an unrecognizable, but angelic voice that resonated from the opposite end of the room. The voice overtook my attention almost immediately, which was fixated on the fluorescent glare produced by the ceiling lights above. New smells, new environment, new faces, with a list of other stimuli, yet I remained quiet as a mouse. As if I were in some state of tranquility. Wait or could I have just been in confusion from my ever-changing environments. The angelic voice slowly approached, then from one warm crevice to another; there I was being exchanged into the arms of yet another unfamiliar face. Six months into my life's journey and there it was I was finally matched!

HOME SWEET HOME

PART II

CHAPTER 5
CHOICE

> "MAY YOUR CHOICES REFLECT YOUR HOPES, NOT YOUR FEARS
> -NELSON MANDELA

If there is one thing that I have learned over the years from being adopted, is that no life, upbringing or journey is perfect. Here I am years later analyzing all that I've experienced after countless years of avoidance and suppression. Stumbling upon the one commonality that unites us all and stretches across the board for each of us "Struggle". Struggle seems to infiltrate itself right into existence of all walks of life, adopted or not. We all face some form of struggle in life, but one thing is for certain; how we choose to view these struggles determines our direction. "We have choice." This overly simplistic statement holds the power to radically transition choice into action, then converting action into tangibility.

Being that our brain functions similar to a circuit switch, we have the capability to toggle between the on or off features of choice. When we make a choice with conviction, subsequently we embody the belief and actions to produce desired results. Along my journey, I had to make a deliberate choice, not to be a victim to the circumstances of being adopted, unwanted and given up at birth. Once in motion I remained in motion, repelling external forces that could possibly impede or hinder progression, as Newton's 1st law of motion states.

I can vividly recall one significant choice that inspired change, that till this day has remnants in my existence. It happened to be the day prior to my first 15-month deployment to Iraq. My mother walks into the bedroom and hands me a book titled "The Purpose Driven Life". First impression was, really mom; right now at this moment? My thoughts were everywhere, but I was trying not to expose my emotions of fear to my mother. I was a soldier, rough, rugged

CHOICE

and emotionally tough; so at least that's what I told myself. The interesting title along with my mom's version of a synopsis, didn't suppress my wondering thoughts enough to become even slightly interested. The following day, on the 22hr aircraft ride is when I would read the book in its entirety. Back then I was far from what one would consider an avid reader, so this wasn't typical behavior. I definitely didn't pick up the book with the intent of it dramatically affecting my life. In all honesty, at that moment my only thoughts were to read just enough to be able to articulate certain parts of the book to my mother. I pealed the cover back, dove in and began reading the first couple of pages. Immediately I was intrigued, completely forgetting that I was even on an aircraft traveling to an imminent war zone. With that aside and off my mind, here I am page after page after page, thumbing through and absorbing this frame shifting information. The chapter began with a profound and thought provoking question that caught my attention "What on earth am I here for"? I started connecting the dots, correlating the message of the chapters with that of my own life. Once I finished the book, I found myself just sitting there with the book in hand, in rumination, processing what I just read.

Fortunately, that was the day I realized I held possession of the ultimate living, breathing and conceptualizing organ. Of course I knew I had a powerful mind, but not to the extent in which I realized during this in-depth self-analyzing session. You mean to tell me my most valuable asset, my personal genie, my brain, my mind, the "control center of my existence", I control and have 24-hour access to that magnitude of power? I was completely dumbfounded, because just a few hours prior, I didn't fully comprehend nor could I effectively describe the mind's extraordinary capabilities. Wait correction; I didn't fully comprehend the depths in just one reading, but I struck oil in terms of at least grasping an idea of the endless possibilities. The choice was mine, what I did from here on out was undeniably in my hands. I had the choice to make proper usage of the sagacity obtained, or to treat it as I did with previous information that had been obtained and not used to my benefit.

> "The difference between happy and unhappy, is choice"
>
> BYRON WESLEY

Years later with countless hours of psychoanalysis and the pursuit of studies in neuroscience, the curiosity continued. The minds inner workings had me hooked, it was as if the light bulb never switched off. Awakened in new depths to this amazing attribute and self-editing feature called consciousness, which provides the capability of choice. Hmm, choice is so much bigger then the six characters used to represent it and make up its phonetics. Choice is essential to the quality, sustainability, fulfillment and continuation of life. Knowing that we possess this powerful cognitive ability, grants us access to levels of life that were once considered off limits. We come fully equipped to choose the direction or destination we travel. Whether it's life, happiness, mental solitude or death, despondency and mental entrapment, the choice is ours. A concept many others and myself have taken far too lightly. It makes you take a step back to ponder on the amount of power we literally walk around with on a second by second basis. Sometimes taking a step back to see the grand scale of things allows us to put things into perspective. So, the idea that we govern each facet of our life is no secret; but to the extent in which we blossom is choice.

CHOICE

THE LIFE ALTERING INTERVIEW...

This interview began just like any other; we exchanged greetings with one another and sat down in our corresponding seats. Before I could formulate my questions according to my interview protocol, he bluntly asked me "if I were affected by adoption?" Again, before I could formulate my response, he took it amongst himself to mention how far he'd come. He went on detailing the daily struggle he'd dealt with pertaining to his inferiority complex, stemming from his adoption. I could hear the level of excitement registering in his voice as he continued expressing his accomplishment. There was one word during his elaboration that struck home "Choice."

After letting him complete his thoughts, I asked him what impact did "Choice" have on his journey? With intense eye contact, he replied in a stern tone "everything". I was conversing with an individual that at one point in life was contemplating suicide, due to internalized feelings of inferiority. Battling high levels of anger, depression and guilt, to the extreme where he felt as if there was no other way out. That reoccurring thought of "what did I do for my parents to give me up?" Loosing grip of life, everything started spiraling. Personal relationships of any sort were none existent, due to the fear of not being good enough and accepted by peers.

Unable to hold a stable place of employment, he quickly turned to other resources for acquiring money, which led him to the judicial system. Daily fights, sexual encounters, drug abuse, multiple failed suicidal attempts and yet here this man sits in front of me illustrating this account of his breathtaking story. After the third suicidal attempt, he found himself on the floor in the prison's library. Opening his eyes and fixating his vision on this tan, green and brown colored book, titled "The Purpose Driven Life".

Yes the exact same life-altering book that I read on my 22hr aircraft ride to Iraq. I didn't interrupt, even though I desperately wanted to, but didn't want to impede his train of thought. He didn't read it initially; it was the third time he came into contact with the book that had him in a state of awe. Giving me a sensational chill, he said "that book exposed me to choice." That was the day he decided to seek the necessary guidance to rid him of those life-debilitating emotions and replace them with invigorating emotions. Not as easy as it sounds, but possible, it is. It took constant dedication, with the willingness to overcome and to live a life filled with purpose and intent.

> "Residing in a place of comfort is the antagonist to our growth and poison to our potential"
> — BYRON WESLEY

MINDSET OF CHOICE...

In order to facilitate the awareness of *"Choice"* we must adopt and commit to an augmented mindset. Being present within our thoughts and actions, understanding stressors and analyzing our finding. Experiment with protocols until a suitable process is found that works effectively. Even moving in incremental steps beyond our behavioral comfort zones, requires innate mental strength. There is neither success nor growth without sacrifice.

Questioning the way we think, allows us the choice and control over our actions. Separating us away from the old and ineffective ways creates a new level of opportunity to commit to. There is absolutely no growth within the comfort, therefore the comfort zone may feel safe, secure and welcoming, but truth is; it doesn't have our best interest in mind. Residing in a place of comfort is the antagonist to our growth and poison to our potential. We protect our comfort zones with excuses, fear and procrastination or as we love to refer to them as "reasons or rationalizations". Recall the last "reason or rationalization" you've told yourself that's prevented you from leaving that self-imposed comfort zone or accomplishing a desired goal. Have you thought about it? Great! Stop, self-sabotage by succumbing to mental imprisonment. We could choose to allow circumstances to dictate our trajectory in life or take the path of resistance to success. Remember we're on a mission to become, not remain and the choice belongs to us.

CHAPTER 6
THE TRANSFORMATION

Once committed to the choice of change, the journey of enlightenment would shift into the next phase. For me, my transformation was inspired through exposure from personal experiences; such as books, articles, positive influences, and sheer enlightenment to the possibilities of life. In light of it all, I've come to the conclusion that one of life's most perpetuating facets or potentialities is when we encounter transformational moments. You know when life presents those life altering decisions aka the crossroad(s) or the fork in the road that can literally change the entire direction of life; yes...those. This is exactly where possibility and choice seamlessly fuse together, disguising itself to the unaware eye as an obstacle, but to the optimistic and trained eye it appears as an opportunity.

> "PERSONAL TRANSFORMATION CAN AND DOES HAVE GLOBAL EFFECT"
> -Marianne Williamson

Reviewing the consensus after conducting over 200 interviews and analyzing the data, there were four emotional states common to a large percentage of the interviewees. Resentment, rejection, inferiority complex and a sense of abandonment seemed to top the list. I began to breakdown and dissect my emotions correlated with my biological parents giving me up for adoption. I knew one thing for sure, I didn't want a life comprised of emotions associated with imbedded resentment, anger or anything closely related. Living in these unresolved emotional states would only foster a damaged self-esteem, frustration, emptiness and or depression. Neither one of those mentioned, fit the sought after life we deserve. Instead, allow life to be filled with abundance of love, awareness, acceptance and confidence. Utilizing the lifestyle we desire as fuel to accelerate towards positivity, enrichment and a healthy paradigm on life. By making this conscious and deliberate decision, we orient our journey in a direction that will generate a collision with greatness. The momentum of awareness will not only began to forcefully shift current patterns of thinking, but will also provoke excitement about the possibilities that were once unknown.

This is exactly what's needed in order to build that extraordinary life; many of us have laid in bed countless nights dreaming about! It's absolutely magical being aware and exercising this phenomenon. Developing an intimate bond with life, but also accepting the accountability and uniqueness associated with knowing that "Our journey is our journey". Yours belonging to you and mine belonging to me. I'm referring to the good, the bad, the beautiful and the ugly. With knowing this vital piece of information, comes the ability to create our journey as we envision or recklessly drive it into a ditch.

> "Before the site of change, the arrival of awareness must present itself"
> — BYRON WESLEY

I JUST WANT TO BE HAPPY...

There was one interviewee in particular that left a profound mark on me with a simplistic, yet thought evoking statement. "I just want to be happy" which she uttered underneath her breath. Her face, stained in sincerity with our eyes locked as if we were engaged in a stare off. She paused for a moment; the room fell silent enough for me to hear her take a single gulp, as she swallowed. I didn't want to interrupt her thought process, so I remained quiet as the room filled with anticipation. What would she follow that statement with, I asked myself? This interview spotlighted a destitute of happiness, but a request to be freed from the chains of anger, guilt and disappointment. She continued going further into detail, mentioning the need to transition out of this emotional state. "I just want to be happy," she clearly stated this time, looking down at the table, with trembling legs.

We finished the session with me assigning her some homework. The assignment was to draw a straight line down her notebook paper, creating two symmetrical halves. One column would be titled "Current Me" and the other column would be titled "New Me". In the "Current Me" column the objective was to write down all the current emotions and lingering thoughts. Addressing both negative and positive. Since we want to go line by line determining what's staying and what needs to go. Basically, identifying all of her strengths and all of her weaknesses. So, as you could imagine in the "New Me" column was where she would literally recreate herself. She would keep traits that she admired from the "Current Me" column, but also adding the updated version of her desired lifestyle. Here is where she'd be tapping into her limitless imagination that had once been oppressed by a belief of inferiority, guilt and anger. Needless to say I was requesting her to come back mentally exhausted; not looking for superficial or "at the surface" answers. If change was going to occur and negative self-imagery be extinguished, these answers needed to shake her existence and come from a place of visceral consideration.

This assignment mimics the vision board concept, where you consolidate your aspirations onto a board and hang it in a highly visible location. This paper would be hung in a manner that would be visible multiple times a day. This primes the mind to focus on the emotional aspirations in the "New Me" column. By constant and repetitive exposure to the written list, you forcefully introduce a new way of thinking into your mundane lifestyle. This daily reoccurrence becomes a positive yet radiant habit over time, while the negative habits listed in the "Current Me" column becomes extinguished. As she returned with the assignment in hand along with a smile extending from ear to ear, indicating that progress had already begun. I quickly joined in on the expression of happiness. Listening to the progression as she elaborated, I couldn't help but smile on the inside while she disclosed her progress.

Feeling empathetic as if it were my own list, nostalgic emotions set in as I reverted back to the day I created and conducted the assignment on my self. Reflecting allowed me to share my experiences, which somehow pushed us into the possibilities of the future. Both of us on the verge of a life lesson, with pen and pad in hand ready to extrapolate the message that was being given by life itself. Its been said, "When the student is ready the teacher appears". Fully cognizant and a student to life; desiring more, refusing to allow history, negative thoughts and uncertainties to become destiny. So to each of us I ask the question, if we're hearing and seeing all of these amazing possibilities of life, why wouldn't we also desire these amazing possibilities our self? So this led me to term the phrase ***"Transformational Moments."***

TRANSFORMATIONAL MOMENTS...

This adventure we all call life, can't be placed on autopilot and expected to deliver us at the doorstep of our destination. This highly intricate system "Life" comes with its own version of what we would consider hiccups, roller coasters and obstacles. Its not always smooth, it's speeds up, slows down, goes up, comes down, turns left and turns right at times when we're simply trying to continue straight. Is that the underlying beauty, behind the inevitable changes presented by life? Life promises unanticipated moments that are uniquely and undeniably tailored to each of us. Example, have you ever experienced this rare, but unmistakable sensation, where you've felt as if life were about to take a drastic turn for the better or for the worst? If not all, a large portion of us has felt this indescribable sensation at some point during our life span.

Usually accompanied with one or more emotional sensation(s) such as butterflies that navigate throughout the stomach cavity, nervousness, anxiety or expectancy! Causing the body to undergo biological responses like a rush of adrenaline, increased heart rate and we can't forget the visible indicators like moist palms and the sweaty forehead. This is a "Transformational Moment" and what I described is the body's emotional and physical expression of it. The body is intentionally informing us that an opportunity is available and at our disposal. This isn't to be taken lightly nor for granted, these opportunities produce enormous levels of potential that if harnessed, can catapult our life toward possibilities and heights in which we've only dreamt of. This requires an elevated version of the "self", the person we are currently; isn't sufficiently fit to take potential to it's optimal altitude. What I mean by this is in order to acquire and reach new heights in life we must undergo a set of life altering transformations that shape and redesign our existence; in a sense making us new. Every next level of life will demand a different you.

> "The desire a person seeks, requires movement beyond where you are now to obtain"
> — BYRON WESLEY

MEDIA GIANT...

There is a media giant that we all know to well, who has evolved into not only a household name and icon, but also one of world's most notable philanthropist, talk show host, executive television producer, chairwoman, TV Network owner and Film actress. We hear of the charitable donations, positive influence and impact she imprints onto diverse communities worldwide. Originally named "Orpah", but family persistently called her Oprah who we now know today as "Oprah Winfrey". Her journey didn't begin with the glitter and glam we see today; there were no flashing camera's, red carpets, extravagant lifestyles or any amount of nepotism. Her now massive creation of success, wasn't inherited or stumbled upon, but built from turning unfortunate moments into triumphant accomplishments. I say unfortunate due to Oprah's grim, dark and desolate beginnings.

Born in Kosciusko, Mississippi out of wedlock into an unstable environment, broken home with multiple relocations and living arrangements. Poverty, drugs, promiscuous behavior and molestation became apart of her inimical routine. As if things weren't devastating enough for nine year old Oprah, life as she knew it would be disrupted once again and take a turn for the worse. The relocation to her mother's residence would be one of the most unpleasant experiences not just mentally, but physically and emotionally. A trusted relative and male accomplice sexually abused Oprah repeatedly, while her inattentive mother was occupied. By repeatedly, I mean these acts unsolicited and disturbing advances would continue from the ages of nine to thirteen. The psychological detriment this would cause for anyone is particularly devastating.

Suffering psychologically, this hardship would ignite her promiscuous behavior, as she openly discusses today. As a result of her indiscriminate ways she would conceive at the delicate age of fourteen and deliver a stillborn.

Imagine the roller coaster of emotions, the difficulties, the confusion and how frightening her adolescent years must have been. Consequently, her unfavorable circumstances would greatly contribute to the relentless and unyielding determination, we see present in her today. The combination of her willingness to persevere and her father's commitment toward providing a life filled with sustenance was a force to be reckoned with. In her teenage years he became her much needed disciplinarian and nurturing figure that would set her sails towards greatness. Relocating to Nashville, Tennessee with him, was just the thriving environment Oprah needed, to cultivate her developing skill set and radiating personality. The relinquishing of her self-destructive thoughts and actions, created the essential space for a life filled with prospering intent. Rigorous studying, dedication and applied erudition began a cycle and was the reason for her receiving prestigious awards of all sorts. Ranging from the honor roll to the Emmy awards, not stopping there, she'd continue on to win recital competitions along with winning the tiara at the Miss Black Tennessee beauty pageant.

    At this point Oprah's momentum is that of locomotive at top-speeds, efforts wouldn't cease there. With tremendous grit she would star in a sequence of movies including her debut film "The Color Purple", she was featured on the cover of TIME Magazine, launching Harpo Productions and of course we can't forget about her first nationally syndication, the "Oprah Winfrey Show". She'd continue to find herself in the midst of success becoming the first African American woman billionaire. Surrounding herself with positive influences such as Maya Angelou, her best friend Gayle King, Dr. Phil, and Ellen DeGeneres. I'm a firm believer that we are the top five individuals we habitually associate with. Having a set of positive influences would only aid in the process during transformational moments. They would be there to inspire in the time of need, provide guidance during the confusion, someone to attend life-enriching events with and will lend you a ear when needed. The common denominator we all share with Oprah's triumphant story is that opportunity is born during transformational moments. Any variation in the slightest of a detail of her life and Oprah wouldn't be who she is today; as the same goes for us. I wanted to illustrate that possibility resides in every circumstance of life, whether good or bad.

PAST, PRESENT & FUTURE...

Accepting the past, I know how extremely difficult it could be, but there is reward in doing so. It allows us to overcome grief, anxiety, pain and the sting of missed opportunity. Understand it happen, it's over and it's absolutely nothing we can do to change what has occurred. Analyzing the situation with a positive paradigm and in a healthy manner, provides the opportunity of growth. Learning from the past is beneficial in realizing the potential of happiness always lies ahead. This gives us a sense of hope to look forward to. It's the difference in being caught in a repetitive cycle or creating a new path. Bad things happen, good things happen and great things happen, so accept and appreciate all facets of life for what they are. Some of us have experienced a past that could have easily devoured us, emotionally, mentally and physically. Instead of allowing this to occur, take advantage of the transformational moments presented by life, by utilizing the past as an impetus instead of obstruction. Accepting it, understanding it and learning from it is our price of admission into a realm of sanity.

> "Don't grant your past permission to steal your present and impede your future"
> — BYRON WESLEY

Embrace the present, be mindful of the present and live in the present. It's continuously unfolding with or without our control. With a mindful approach to life "transformational moments are vivid and in abundance. Mindfulness of "transformational moments" in the present, grant us vigilance to our immediate environment, thoughts, emotions and reactions. We must remain cognizant to elicit the best possible outcome, according to our present level of awareness. What we do in the present is in direct proportion to the quality of our future. When "transformational moments" present themselves we must commit to the possibility and see it through.

> "To a mind that is still, the universe reveals it's plans"
>
> BYRON WESLEY

In retrospect, our pursued future was once a present day image, encapsulated within our mind. This informs us that our future has the ability to be shaped directed and facilitated, into a 3dimensional representation; in which we call life. In order to reach the desired 3D destination, we must develop a process in the present that would align us with the results we seek. By consistently evaluating and augmenting this developed process, we're able to monitor proficiency and progression. It won't be easy, obstacles will occur, but don't stress over the future; it hasn't arrived yet. So convert that worrisome energy into focusing on creating the future as you envision. Disengage the autopilot feature; a large percentage of the population has governing their life. Remove the blindfolds and lets take an active approach to designing our future.

> "Predict your future by creating it in the present"
>
> BYRON WESLEY

Optimizing Transformational Moments

To effectively optimize the ramifications of transformational moments, something new and never experienced is required of us. I'm referring to a new level of "self", a paradigm shift and a new self-identity in which we perceive ourselves. These transformational moments require a level of vigor, consistency and resiliency; foreign to the ways we've grown accustomed to. Far to often we're given opportunities for transformation and with in a matter of just hours or days, work ethic drastically diminishes. Why, Is the question that goes unanswered far to often? Could it be due that the level of commitment to the choice of change is ineffective? Put another way, our **"REASON"** just isn't strong enough!

We give up due to our insignificant **"REASON"**. By connecting the **"REASON"** to something bigger than our self, this simply applies a higher sense of responsibility. This method ensures the highest form of commitment to see the behavior, task or overall goal through to its completion. Take the slender built woman weighing roughly around 115 pounds soaking wet. She witnessed a stranger being struck by an oncoming vehicle to then get pinned underneath the tire of the vehicle. What happen next was astonishing, that left onlookers completely baffled with her spontaneous actions and hysterical strength. Immediately without contemplation, she sprinted to the vehicle and to the amazement of all, she raised the automobile. Just enough to free the confined stranger, who today is forever thankful for her courageous act. This is not seen under normal circumstances, the brain has this automatic response feature that unleashes superior mental and physical capabilities.

    I say all of this to say, when the **"REASON"** is bigger than oneself these heroic like mental capabilities are made available for our beneficial use. If you find yourself affected by behavioral inconsistencies and are aware of them; that's perfect! You're on your way to forever resolving this challenge, by shifting your **"REASON"**. For transformational longevity, fasten your seat belt and prepare for the rollercoaster ahead. Regression in areas that require above average action can no longer be a factor, no more excuses, reasons or rationalizations. Fully commit to immense positive actions such as, habitual self investing, associating with positive influences, building great habits, pursing goals, managing moods, exercising strengths and converting weaknesses into strengths. By taking necessary action in these areas increase the probability of obtaining and maintaining the longevity of your achievement. At this level of commitment, greatness becomes default and second nature. The highway to longevity is a choice that is up to you and I. Find a **"REASON"** that specifically works for you and optimizes your transformational moment!

CHAPTER 7
MY JOURNEY IS MY JOURNEY

It's absolutely amazing, just how intricate and personalized each of our life's are. Traveling our individualized paths, at different times, unequal speeds, descending

> "SOME SAY IT'S ALL ABOUT THE JOURNEY, WHILE OTHERS SAY IT'S ALL ABOUT THE DESTINATION; I SAY IT'S ABOUT BOTH"
> -BYRON WESLEY

to unusual depths and even ascending to various heights. This uniqueness creates diversity that spans from one region of the world to another. The beauty of diversity intertwines our paralleled paths, picking up many heart-felt stories, experiences and conflicting perspectives. Believe it or not, this adds value that we are able to draw from or discard. In life, I take the position that there are no accidents, just lessons. This optimistic approach unlocks the potential for growth and learning, in every circumstance of life. That's not to say that difficult and challenging childhoods of any sort, can't take a toll on even the strongest of individuals.

I've not only seen it, but also dealt with the oppression first hand, so I know the level of fight required to overcome. Motherless, unwanted and being raised in a broken home comes with a multitude of struggles. The secret is whatever the struggle maybe; we don't have to live in it. Stand up and fight, because the challenge isn't bigger than us, we are stronger, smarter and faster than any obstacle that can be placed on our path. If left unaddressed it could result in psychologically deficits and untoward emotions. It is completely natural to consider our fight; more complicated and complex than that of the person you are comparing it to. Maybe it could be our limited frame of reference in which we draw from. Hear me out, how many times have you seen, read, or heard about another individual's journey that immediately made you reconsider just how bad or good your life was? I know I've experienced it numerous times. Learning that exposure and interaction with others, helps us realize every life is filled with some good and some bad. What is good and bad? It's based off our perception, which is shaped through motivations, morals, cultures, religions and conditioning. Our world is, as we perceive it, which explains the phenomena of how two individuals raised in the same scenario can have opposing views. Yes for those alike and myself, many would consider our existence a misfortune, adverse and unfavorable, but for me; it's simply a journey. Acknowledging the unpredictable nature of a journey, we quickly realize how unique and uncertain they have the tendency to be. Embrace the uncertainty, the biggest rewards are granted to those who take risky action toward the unknowns. If we don't take decisive action, how will we ever achieve our goals, reach total self-confidence or the emotional status we are in search for?

MY JOURNEY IS MY JOURNEY

> "This customizable journey we call life, will be met with opposition"
>
> **BYRON WESLEY**

THE STRONGEST TREE...

During a thunderstorm nebulous clouds produce adverse winds, lighting filled skies followed by ground rattling and thunderous roars. Once the inhospitable weather passes, the weaker, less rugged rubbish is uprooted and scattered throughout the forest floor. The mightiest trees and root systems that withstand the strongest winds continue to develop by expanding in girth and increasing their depth of the root system. By doing so, this solidifies their strength and positioning in preparation for uncertainty. The mightiest tree is the best version of me. The best version of myself grows not when the winds are low and the sun is shinning. It's when velocity of the winds increase and the skies turn grey, that I am tested. Essential nourishment is provided during the rainstorm, while thereafter; the sun also delivers its nutrients. These revolving elements produce a cycle crucial to the evolutionary journey of becoming the mightiest tree in the forest. Why would I resist and avoid the strongest storms, if this is the journey of developing into mightiest me? It makes me wonder, shouldn't I be asking the universe for the necessary adversity and uncertainty needed to excel?

Firstly, understanding the definition of adversity as it relates to this message is "in contrary of". So when stepping into resistance and out of comfort, by definition we are going in contrary of what we're accustom to. This concept took time for me to fully grasp it. This was outright mind blowing. I was content and happy especially when the winds were low and the sun was shining. I was culturally conditioned to only ask the universe for smooth and obstacle free days, avoiding resistance at all cost. When in fact, this approach was an impedance, literally stealing my chances of reaching self-reliance. As Tony Robbins profoundly said, "The quality of life is in direct proportion to the amount of uncertainty one can comfortably live with". So, in order to reach new altitudes, I needed to make myself vulnerable to necessary levels of adversity that coincide with my level of desire. I had to continue reaching for the canopies, placing the proper amounts of trust into my abilities. Proving it to myself and myself only that I could walk into the face of opposition and come out mentally stronger. Strengthening my positioning in preparation for longevity, like that of the strongest tree in the forest. Allow the revolving elements required for my mental strengthening and nourishment to present themselves. Relentless rain, the unbarring suns rays and any other crucial element. Roots extended to unknown depths, my branches reaching beyond the canopy towards the stratosphere.

> "I am the strongest tree in the forest"
>
> BYRON WESLEY

This daily affirmation helped solidify my mental foundation, as I continued my transformation. It reinforced my self-confidence, during the periods when reoccurring insecurities crept up. At such a young and impressionable age you could only imagine the direction my thoughts would go. So by creating an affirmation, as I would like you to do as well. We'll be able to disrupt and channel negative energy into positive and reinsuring thoughts. This technique will serve as a mode of motivation and keep your mind surrounded by the thoughts you want in your environment.

I FELT LIKE AN OUTDATED TOY...

After, analyzing the first interview, I found the root cause to her overall message. Presented to me in this almost fluctuant voice, as if she dreaded reaching to the depths of her emotions. It was the initial experience of feeling unwanted. An emotion common to those who have been placed up for adoption experienced a divorce, mentally and physically abused or many other scenarios, that are extremely difficult for children to process. The situation was saddening, but a certain aspect seemed to resonate at a higher frequency with me. She goes on to describe her experience of feeling like an outdated toy that had been decommissioned. This immediately snatched any remaining attention that wasn't already preoccupied. Outdated and decommissioned I repeated to myself, how could a human being compare himself or herself to a toy? As she sat across the table from me with a face stained with pain, anger and resentment, it's as if I felt every ounce of her concealed agony. I had to fight back tears, this was touching beyond expectation. Tears in her eyes fell though, continuously one by one onto her folded hands below. "I don't love" she said, was this in fear of not knowing how and never experiencing it, I asked? "Yes, what if I'm not good at it?" Replying to my question. She explicitly expressed her feelings in detail, which had been bottled up for over 27 years now. I tried to explain the diverse concept of love simplistically, but intentionally informing her of the level of vulnerability needed to experience it. Comparing it to a journey majority of us share as youth, using the analogy of learning how to ride a bicycle. This was an endeavor many children couldn't wait to embark upon. Having to painfully watch from the sideline, as the older kids gracefully race up and down the streets on their bikes. There was a starting point to achieving this, just as there is for everything in life. The end goal was remaining upright, hair blowing in the wind and riding flawlessly off into the sunset with friends, without the trainings wheels. Before that is made tangible, we would approach the bicycle with a level of convection, believing it is possible. The idea of falling, scrapped knees and banged up elbows isn't even on your mind, being that this is your first attempt with the training wheels removed. Grab the handle bar; pull the bike towards you with your instructor present to hold you upright as you climb aboard. 1,2,3 you're pushed forward, and just as fast as you counted to 3 you're on the ground, contemplating whether or not this is a good idea. The scraps, the bruises and the idea of quitting have set in, but you don't because the beauty of the outcome outweighs it all. So brushing your knees off and getting back on is your final choice. After countless attempts and many injuries later, you're successful, upright and headed towards the makeshift finish line at the end of the block.

We must make ourselves vulnerable to the elements of life, in order to even consider reaping the benefits of what we seek. Susceptibility is apart of the process, give yourself to that in, which you seek. How could we learn to ride a bicycle if we don't make ourselves vulnerable to scraps, bruises and falls? Exact same concept when applied to love, we'll never love if we don't attempt to love, we'll never succeed if we don't make mistakes. Learning to look at vulnerability in this perspective changes everything while in the pursuit of fulfillment, I told her. Wrapping up the interview I reinsured myself that my journey wasn't the best and wasn't necessarily the worst either, despite what my pondering mind would lead me to think. It was evident; she had taken on guilt and developed an inferiority complex. Feeling as if she wasn't deserving of love and companionship. Shuffling through my notes I read her my latest entry titled "Strongest Tree In The Forest". Once I completed reading the entry, she repeated the affirmation at least five to six times "I am the strongest tree in the forest". That was the first time during our interview that I heard an unmistakable boast of confidence. By the end of the interview, I realized just how powerful daily affirmations were to get through troubling times. It wasn't going to be an overnight victory, but progression was made. The avoidance of falling victim to spiraling thoughts was the objective. So with a consistent regiment of seeing her psychologist and our monthly mental reshaping sessions, let's just say my first interviewee has learned to ride the bicycle of love.

> "We must make ourselves vulnerable to the elements of life, in order to even consider reaping the benefits of what we seek"
> -BYRON WESLEY

Three Dynamic E's...

Our quest in life is directly correlated to what I call Three Dynamic E's: ***"Exposure, Education and Execution."*** Neither more important then the other equally valued and extremely intertwined. Each phase is highly accessible and the maneuverability between each is rather easy. Seeds of exposure and education are planted daily, but along with execution of potential; our existence is shaped. Knowing I could only aspire to the level of my awareness, I drastically increased my level of exposure. Once I discovered the dynamic trio, I welcomed and embraced change, being that I knew it brought along "New Experiences." The exposure inspired, while education enlightened and the execution propelled.

I	II	III
EXPOSURE	EDUCATION	EXECUTION

MY JOURNEY IS MY JOURNEY

EXPOSURE:

Exactly what is exposure, Merriam Webster defines it as the fact of experiencing or being affected by something. Agreed, but I have to go a bit deeper and say that it is the gateway into sensation, our dreams, imagination and possibilities. Exposure is experiencing the slightest sensation through any of our 5 empirical senses. Seeing, tasting, feeling, smelling and hearing; each uniquely create new concepts, new ideas and awareness levels for us to draw from. I've yet to experience dreaming beyond my current level of exposure. To the extent in which we are exposed, is the extent in which we can dream. We have an unbecoming tendency to mentally discard information, which contradicts our pre-existing views. While only indulging in information that reinforces pre-existing notions. Why continue this approach of cognitive dissonance, when exposure only expands our narrow and limited views we've placed onto the world? By simply interacting with new people, places and things, we are granted the luxury of contrasting views and reaching cognitive equilibrium. Through traveling we not only experience new cultures, but we taste new foods, observe foreign rituals and witness new ways of the world. Your travel destination doesn't have to be some distant land 1000 miles away; visiting the next town over is enough to expose us to exciting variations. Through my journey of interviews with adopted children and adults, I was exposed to various views, experiences and an array of coping mechanisms. My horizon was broadened, which gave me in depth understanding into the minds of afflicted individuals. Social interactions created therapeutic venting sessions, technique swaps and an environment conducive to positivity. This goes to show the influential affects of how exposure can elicit positive change. There is inspiration to be drawn from every exposure.

MY JOURNEY IS MY JOURNEY

EDUCATION:

Education is beyond the classroom environment or the "traditional educational setting." The universe is our classroom, not just the university. The universe offers so much, literally more than we have the capacity to process and store. Education is the enlightenment to depths of the world. Exposure to enchanting books, articles and lectures fuel the desire to learn. Retaining education through mnemonics makes the process not only enjoyable, but also addictive. The more books or literature we have on a particular topic the deeper our comprehension becomes. The moment I was introduced to my first self help book "The Purpose Driven Life" I fell in love and was instantly hooked. I began exposing myself to every piece of self-help material I could get my hands on. I became a learning machine, with no off switch. Feeding the control center of my existence "my brain" was an investment that I couldn't afford not to invest in. With advancements in technology, finding topics on personal development has never been so accessible.

EXECUTION:

All that we envision, whether it's an imaginative lifestyle or occupational aspirations, they are both direct reflections of our level of exposure and education. **The last component in this trio is Execution.** This phase transforms our planted seeds of potential into tangibility and is brought to life. Even though execution is all that the world sees, planning and strategizing behind the scenes are equally important. Self-reliance is crucial to this phase, which is the ability to depend on our own independence, judgment and resources. I had to identify my overall purpose in life, basically the reinvention of my existence. Once identified, I began to organize, construct and locate proper resources to execute my detailed plan. The way I figured it and you may agree, dreams without execution become nightmares and regrets. I was my only resistance standing between who I am and what I wanted to be. Yes, developing the proper discipline to focus solely on what mattered was challenging. So, once again I increased my level of exposure and education. Expanded my network with top performers, multiplied my arsenal of literature and lastly I executed. Overcoming self imposed resistance through incremental, consistent and effective steps done day in and day out. This was a perfect example of how exposure transposed into knowledge; and understanding into skill set. Each dynamic E plays a pivotal role in the transformation. I started thinking of these transformational moments as spaceships sitting on the launching pad, in count down sequence. Having the capability to exit the stratosphere and discover the next awaiting galaxy or remain stationary, deteriorate and eventually perish. Every aspect working together to lift this 4.4 million pound spaceship into orbit. Our goals are the spaceship, our efforts are the fuel tanks and our execution is the ignition to initiate blast off.

> "Constantly Expose, Constantly Educate and Constantly Execute"
>
> BYRON WESLEY

PART III

CHAPTER 8
REINVENT YOURSELF

Why would we wish for a redo, when everyday is an opportunity to reinvent ourselves? Life provides a constant source for reinvention; I'm not just talking about finding

> "LIFE ISN'T ABOUT FINDING YOURSELF, IT'S ABOUT CREATING YOURSELF"
> -HENRY THOREAU

ourselves. I'm referring to the use of imagination, where we envision our desired self, hit the reset button and completely reinvent our life. Call in the demolition and remodeling crew; it's time to reconstruct. Starting at that faulty foundation, where bad habits, resentment and erroneous self-images reside. Age is not a factor here, but mindset is!

We must rewire our minds and create a new way of thinking, before we can master a new way of being. The mind is fully capable; it's a master of reorganization and mental pruning. The only challenge impeding us from creating the best version of "self" is us. Not society, not the environment, friends, family, government, economy nor the political parties, it's our doing. Allowing feelings of disappointment, hurt, resentment, guilt or whatever afflictive emotion to run rampant is not the way. One of the strongest displays of personal strength is the ability to forgive. This doesn't imply weakness, this suggest mental maturity and sets us free from harvesting negativity. How can we properly reinvent ourselves when we're holding on to damaging pieces? The answer to that very question is the gateway into the abundance of happiness.

Our mundane thoughts and habits contribute a large portion to the success of our happiness or to the continuation of misery. This is the chapter where everything we've discussed thus far, meshes together into one beautiful piece of artwork. Our overall objective is to reinvent and reach total self-confidence, by extracting the unique beneficial qualities we posse. This hand drawn self portrait will be autographed by you, signifying the authenticity and dedication put into this project. Before we start with our customizations, there are few prerequisites to tackle.

> "Adopting the rules of society, is relinquishing freedom of personal autonomy"
> — BYRON WESLEY

BACK AGAINST THE ROPES...

Yes, life can be challenging, which makes conquering milestones even more gratifying upon completion. Each life comes with it's on set of misfortune, these moments cause us to dig deep and I mean deeper than ever before. While digging we'll uncover essential components to our individualized journeys. Though our essential components will differ from person to person, becoming inspired by some one else's "transformational moment" has stood the test of time.

I'm no boxing fanatic, but I remember the significant impact this one particular story had on me. It was the story of Mike Tyson vs. Buster Douglas. By taking bits and pieces from the match, I was able to apply its significance and grab inspiration. Listening to the news reporter as he began to convey why Douglas was the underdog, with absolutely no hopes of winning the match. Due to what should of been an obvious reasons, like Tyson being this undisputed heavy weight champion. This resulting in him having the winning odds stacked in his favor. So as I started analyzing this "match", it was as if a light bulb went off. This match represented my own circumstances, obstacles and challenges that I've faced throughout my life. It was evident; I was Buster Douglas, symbolic to the "underdog" of the story and Tyson would represent the forceful, unfair and unyielding "Life". Yet, it was those last couple seconds of the 8th round, Tyson landed a powerful right uppercut immediately disorienting and knocking Douglas to his knees. It was during Douglas's contact with the canvas that presented the perfect opportunity to recall his "REASON" to get back up. Contributing that reason to the lost of his mother. That inspired him to dig deep and reinvent the trajectory of his current circumstances. Though Tyson had an opposing agenda, his reputation proved that once you were knocked down, there was no return. Resiliency kicked in, Douglas was up, off the canvas with his back against the ropes after a 9-second count shocking the entire world! The highly skilled, aggressive and undefeated perception associated with Tyson would forever change. In the historic 10th round Douglas had a face filled with conviction, connecting an overwhelming uppercut to the face of Tyson. Whiplash was the least of Tyson's concern. Douglas following thru with a combination of blows knocking Tyson down for the first time ever in his career.

I can promise you this; life will push our backs against the rope, eventually knocking us down. The canvas is not where we live, so our only option is to get back up. Our **"Reason"** is stronger than any hit or commentary. Don't ever let anyone, including yourself tell you that something can't be achieved. Never accept the limitations of those who place them upon

REINVENT YOURSELF

themselves. This is an internal battle they are facing and must conquer, that has absolutely nothing to do with you. Imagine if Buster Douglas, the Wright brothers, Steve Jobs, Oprah and Neil Armstrong had listened to the limiting thinking patterns of others. Would you believe me if I suggested that our magnitude of potential far exceeds that of those I just mentioned?

> "Inspiration or desperation are the two reasons we change"
>
> BYRON WESLEY

FORGIVE...

We've all been hurt, mistreated or have experienced betrayal to some degree. Is it a good feeling? Absolutely not, it's painful and unwelcoming. Whether it's from being adopted, which leaves a stain of feeling unwanted and abandoned or being abused mentally, physically or emotionally. Some individuals initially express disbelief that aggression, frustration, or mistrust could surface from unresolved life experiences. When left unresolved these individuals are prone to having anxiety disorders, mood disturbances or substance abuse disorders. Becoming aware and acknowledging the painful circumstance, creates an opportunity for forward progression. Coming to terms with the past, accepting that it's happened and it cannot be changed shifts our mentality from victim to liberation. This produces a shift in attitude, which places us in a position of power to oversee and extract knowledge from the experience. A mentality of this caliber places all responsibility onto us, to control what happens next in our life. This is an opportunity to take life by the horns and reinvent life as we see necessary. Having the proper attitude is crucial to forgiveness, being that our attitude determines our direction. There are many ways to express emotional pain, but we must remain mindful to ensure they are advantageous to our health. Forgiving promotes a sense of happiness, stronger immune system and improved heart health. Where, holding on to pain, resentment and betrayal quickly becomes debilitating and fosters a list of adverse affects. Some such as low self-esteem, depression, stress, hostility and anxiety. Give up the need for revenge by disarming negative thoughts. Harvesting hatred is conducive to a victim mentality. No one can

can emotional hurt us unless we grant them the permission to. The emotional agony begins once we start replaying the traumatic incident over and over in our heads. We prolong and magnify the hurt by placing the burning memories onto a mental treadmill. Ok, we were hurt, but we survived, so holding on to resentment is no longer an option. I'm sure we can all agree that this is a healthy approach to living a blissful life. So then why is it so difficult for us to relinquish resentment and grant forgiveness? As we discussed in previous chapters, the path of least resistance is usually the most attractive, yet the least rewarding. It's easy to conform to anger, lash out in hostility and remain vindictive. Makes us feel strong and in control, but in reality we are letting go of self-control. Now it's when we lean into the discomfort of opposition to forgive, that life begins to illuminate and take shape. I'll be honest, forgiving isn't for the weak hearted and those who aren't up for a fight. For those individuals willing to roll up the sleeves and double knot your sneakers, this reinvention challenge is for us. By accepting the reality of the incident and forgiving, we are finding a way to live in resolve. Forgiveness isn't implying that, their actions were okay, but rather:

- I respect my health and well-being to the upmost.
- I grant myself the inner serenity necessary for a healthy lifestyle and mindset.
- This doesn't mean I need to deliver an apology.
- I understand it won't immediately erase the sentiment about the situation.
- It doesn't mean everything is now okay.

By forgiving we are doing ourselves a service; this is not for the other person. Create a mindset of gratitude by being thankful for who and what we do have. Focusing on the positive things in life helps us realize just how much we have to be thankful for.

FORGIVENESS WORKSHEET

1. **What angered you?** Acknowledge the reality of the incident and the emotional affect you've experienced.

2. **Analyze the experience.** "What doesn't kill you only makes you stronger." Open the range of your mind, be able to articulate what has affected you! Is there something about yourself you've learned during this incident?

3. **Focus on healing.** Gain the proper attitude. Refuse being a victim, release the hurt and focus on the future. Mediate, indulge in positivity and create ideal environments.

4. **Commit to change.** The objective is happiness anything that conflicts; remove it. You are priority!

FORGIVENESS WORKSHEET

What angered you?

What have you learned from this experience about yourself?

What would you like this pain to turn into?

Describe how you would refocus your energy towards your future & purpose in life?

REINVENT YOURSELF

happiness is an attitude of the mind. I've learned that the individual defines his or her happiness. What makes me happy may very well leave you in a state of upset and discontentment. This opens opportunity to create individualized definitions of happiness, in order to live in alignment with our values and beliefs. We are known to reach the highest levels of happiness when we live life on our own terms. Reshaping the way happiness is looked at, provides endless possibility of reinvention.

So take me for example, given up for grabs, motherless at one point, placed for adoption and growing up with no father. I had the choice to live in the agony of feeling unworthy or completely reinvent life and happiness on my terms. I knew that during the pursuit of my ideal self, challenges would emerge, but happiness lied on the other side and that was my only focus. Equipped with tunnel vision, I set out on this journey in search for happiness. I found it, but what my discovery revealed would forever reshape my paradigm on happiness. Here I am overcoming struggles, knocking down barriers and tackling self imposed limitations. Just to realize this innate emotion I've searched high and low for, has been within me since the beginning of my life's journey. I went on a search for something that was already inside of me, literally within me every single moment of the day. Being completely oblivious to its presence put me on what seemed to be a never-ending treadmill.

This would be equivalent to attending a community function, unaware of the reason for the gathering. You're handed an empty basket with minimal instruction to go out into the open yard and fill the basket. The rest of the group is given detailed instruction, it's Easter and they're on the hunt for colorful designed eggs. The yard is filled with an abundance of Easter eggs and decoy objects. While outside you come into contact with a million and one objects, unsure as to what to place into your basket. Everyone reenters the building, dumping the baskets onto the counter revealing the contents. The group's counter is filled with an array of colorful designed Easter eggs. Your pile is composed of rocks, bottle caps, foliage, and coins. Point being, we won't find what we aren't looking for. The group's mind was primed to search for one specific item and was successful at completing the task. On the other hand not being mentally primed, you unmindfully collected objects at will.

Let our minds be conditioned to locate happiness, despite what we are experiencing and we will locate it. Eventually, it will become apart of the mundane routine, being that our mind is a creature of habit. What we seek is seeking us, put another way we find what we are looking for. This shows that not only inspiration can be plucked from anything, but so can happiness. Like myself many of us will go our entire existence in search for this indigenous feeling of pleasure and enjoyment. How many times have you heard phrases similar to these "If only I were this or looked like that or could have these things, I'd be happy"? When in fact, tapping into mindfulness places us in the present, allowing us to acknowledge how far we've come. While in pursuit of hopes, dreams and aspirations we must not forget our significance. Be happy while in pursuit. Take a moment to stop everything and show gratitude to our current progress. No matter how grand or insignificant you find it to be, its progress!

HAPPINESS WORKSHEET

1. **Define your Happiness.** Create a definition of what happiness means to you! Remember, we cannot find what we aren't looking for. Once we know "our" definition of happiness, this now becomes our foundation to living life on our terms!

2. **Live in Gratitude.** Living in gratitude not only cultivates positive emotion, but also possess this life transforming quality. Intentionally look around and, observe that there is so much to be grateful for and aware of. Remaining attentive allows us to extract satisfaction from every circumstances and overall increases our happiness.

HAPPINESS WORKSHEET Cont'd

3. **Challenge Yourself.** Take gratitude walks, acquire accountability partners and surround yourself with positive influence. Happiness doesn't occur on its own - it's when we challenge ourselves to think, plan and execute. This assembles our self-efficacy and pushes the envelope on goal setting. Taking accountability for life, places the power in our hands to create the necessary change.

4. **Control your Switch.** Learn to activate your "Happy Switch" by counteracting negativity with methods of mindfulness, meditation or yoga. This promotes overall serenity and long-lasting happiness.

HAPPINESS WORKSHEET

Define what happiness means to you?

Make a list of what you're grateful for?

Choose from a range of activities designed to relax the mind including gratitude walks, reading, meditation, exercise, etc..

Activate your mindfulness "Switch." Daily jot down how you interpret and react to what's happening in your mind. (Judgement Free)

REINVENT YOURSELF

HABITS...

Let's talk about habits; how this six lettered word is at the foundation of our personal development or at the root of our self-destruction. Habits are the integral building blocks of our existence. They make up who we are, what we desire, when, where and how we utilize our day. They are the mundane and involuntary activities in which we do with minimal conscious thought. These almost mindless behaviors eliminate the need for immense mental processing, so our minds can concentrate on higher-level cognition. For example, take the all so common and widely discussed habits within personal hygiene. From a time long before we can vividly recall, we've been conditioned to practice proper habits of hygiene. The amount of concentration required during the learning stages, were rather meticulous. Whether it was countless hours dedicated to potty training, bathing properly or learning how to brush our teeth.

We weren't born with know how of completing these task, we had to learn them.

These soon to be daily habits took time, concentration and repetition, before they could be performed as effortlessly as they are today. Learning to hold the toothbrush with one hand, while accurately dispensing the correct amount of toothpaste with the opposite hand, took practice. Starting at the front of the mouth maneuvering our way towards the back, ensuring each tooth was vigorously brushed. All of this while maintaining our balance on a stepping stool to reach the mirror. We had to be attentive to every stroke; our minds were solely focused on the task at hand. Today minimal focus is needed to perform any of these hygienic tasks. Why, because with constant repetition these behaviors have become programmed. Basically, automatic which sets us on autopilot. Being that we are creatures of habit, our programmable minds have this highly adaptive and malleable function to it. What we repeatedly do becomes so deeply wired into our minds that we'd continue a behavior that produces unfavorable results. This is the amount of power we allow habits to have over our lives. Our subconscious mind doesn't discriminate against the character of a habit. Good or bad, our radar is on a constant hunt for repetitive activity lurking within our environment to convert it into a habit.

Fortunately, this radar could be used to our advantage, by honing in on advantageous behaviors. Like practicing daily affirmations, positive self-talk and reading daily. This also permits us to hone in on adverse behavior that needs eliminating. Though these may seem like small and insignificant adjustments, they have the ability to revolutionize our life. It wont be instant gratification or an overnight process, but gradually I can promise habits will begin to form. Eventually shifting our focus from the actual task or behavior to a more instinctive, natural and automatic approach. Here is our opportunity to reconstruct our foundation and reinvent life. By engaging our radar, we can target habits and evaluate whether or not they are conducive to our overall goals. Grouping habits into two categories simplifies the reorganization process, where they fall into either the "Anchor or Engine Classification". Just what is this Anchor or Engine classification?

Anchor or Engine...

Ok, so let's take a 20,000 to 60,000 ton cruise ship, with massive propellers powered by diesel electric engines. Enough momentum is created to match that of multiple freight trains. Speeds reaching above 31 knots allowing the vessel to gracefully glide through the ocean. Practically unstoppable in this form, but add an anchor to the equation and the dynamics suddenly change. With the anchor being only a fraction of the ships size, how on earth does it prevent movement? Two hook like flukes penetrate the seabed and forcefully embed themselves at an angle. If anchoring firmly secures a colossal cruise ship in place, imagine the effect anchors would have in our life. We are that massive cruise ship, we're fully equipped with a powerful diesel engine and the ability to control our anchoring habits.

The habits that no-longer serve us purpose, act as anchors that we allow to interfere with pursuing our potential. While our beneficial habits have the potential and power of a diesel engine on full throttle. Simplify the categorization process, by placing habits in their respective category. Either Anchor or Engine, those are the only two categories; no room for error nor confusion. If the habit doesn't propel you toward your desired goals it's an Anchor. Habitual behaviors that slow you down, impede progression or cause harm belong in the anchor pile. Here is where they will be compiled, incinerated and discarded all together. Why climb the mountain of life with unnecessary baggage?

We were born with instincts, but not habits, somewhere along our journey we learned these self-defeating behaviors meaning we can also reprogram and unlearn them. Procrastination, self doubt, fear of change, fear of rejection, lacking accountability for success or failure, drinking or remaining in negative environments are just a few Anchoring habits that won't propel us towards our true happiness. Cue, routine and reward make up the vicious cycle of bad habits, that stops today! Extinguishing the targeted habit will require more than our awareness and persistence. When trying to extinguish an unwanted or damaging habit we often strategize about will power, motivation and self-control factors. Instead what if we began implementing ways on how to set up new and beneficial habits to replace the old and inadequate ones? This exposes us to new routines, people, places and cues. Creating room for life altering reinvention!

This brings me to the "Engine" category, where great behaviors develop into distinguished habits. Habits categorized here, grant us the ability to enjoy the ride on cruise-control. How exhilarating does life become when we are happily involved in positive, life enriching and progressive activity? Our habits are like the massive blades and diesel engine of the cruise ship, while in motion they propel and create an unstoppable momentum. These are the activities that overtime, begin to form life-altering patterns. Shaping the foundation in which we operate daily. Accelerating us in the direction we desire in life. These are the chariots to health, happiness and well-being. Habits like meditating, practicing mindfulness, exercise, daily affirmations, being grateful, taking accountability, writing goals and pursuing goals have a direct influence on our progression in life. With repetition these propelling habits become self-perpetuating and automatic. Since we have the choice in which habits we habituate to, why not program the ones in alignment with our aspirations? Make health, happiness and well-being not only a priority, but a habit as well!

HABIT MODIFICATION WORKSHEET

1. Becoming Aware. Identify the *"Anchoring Loop"* This loop consist of the Stimulus, Behavior, and the Reward. The stimulus is the trigger that sets this repetitive behavior in motion. Identify what is at end of loop also known as the reward. This is the reason **WHY** you continue to repeat the behavior. Now it's time to reverse engineer.

2. The Replacement. Here is where we switch the *Anchor* with the *Engine*. That anchoring habit is controlled by you and now is the time we retire it. Before we construct a plan and write it all down, lets begin to visualize the longterm success of this swap.

3. The Plan. This highly adaptive organ known as our brain comes hardwired to habituate. Now, we just have to give it a plan to habituate to! We can now convert our *visualization* into written instruction in checklist format. The point of having a checklist is to progressively check off box's and track the process. Lets break down our plan into manageable chunks and execute.

4. Celebrate your Success. We are *"result seeking"* creatures, let's feed that guilty pleasure by celebrating the small gains. This keeps us excited about the progress and motivated on the bigger picture.

HABIT MODIFICATION WORKSHEET

What Anchoring habit(s) do you want to modify?

Visualize the amazing lifestyle change after switching out the Anchor with the Engine; (Describe it)

I plan to replace my old [Anchor] habit with my new [Engine] habit by...

Describe how you plan to celebrate each of your small gains?

REINVENT YOURSELF

KEYSTONE CONCLUSION...

I know that adoption has changed my life, along with my mother and every individual that I've come in contact with. I absolutely love the idea of being chosen and taken care of the best way my mother knew how. A lot of my early beginning experiences remain a mystery and allow me to fantasize on an array of possibilities. Yes I could dwell on the negative aspects of adoption, like being abandoned, feeling as if I wasn't good enough and the list continues. That is the recipe for downward spiraling or creating a course of self-destructing thoughts. I'd rather not take that route, knowing that the outcome of life is completely my responsibility. Instead I extract positivity from every situation I encounter; no it doesn't shelter me from negativity. It does allow me to spot the inconspicuous gems known as opportunities in every situation. I had to intentionally decide that I was going to make the best life possible. It was easy for me to proclaim, not knowing the intricacies involved with manifesting such grand desire. Starting with adjustments in thinking, environments, associates and influences the extraordinary journey began. I totally underestimated the amount of action and effort needed to accomplish such endeavor. Embracing change was one of the most difficult tasks I've ever encountered, but by far the most rewarding. Learning that the only adversary was my mind, gave new light unto how I viewed the inevitable challenges of change. This journey has allowed me to develop my own identity, teaching me to be proud of who, what, when, where and how you've come about. This book was a combination of my life and other adopted individuals. We wanted to share our journey in hopes of inspiring any and every individual that came into contact with this book. Not only sharing the success but the challenges faced as well.

REINVENT YOURSELF

During multiple of my interviews, discussing the "Anchor vs. Engine" technique seemed effective in acknowledging, evaluating and categorizing habits. After just a couple days of tracking habitual patterns, the group returned with a highly organized and categorized list. Bringing exposure to habits, under the titles "Anchors or Engine." This created the necessary awareness to begin the radical transformation of implementing new routines and upgraded daily habits. Truly comprehending that anything done daily would eventually become habitual. Vulnerability to positive influences such as people and environments created access to new concepts to draw from. Shinning spotlights on areas of life, which have been dormant far to long. This exposed the level of customization available within our life. With the groups advancing mindset, the possibilities became evident and the desire to discard damaging habits increased. In life majority of us know what habits need changing. Lets not wait any longer, for consequences to continue to compound. For those who aren't really sure which habits need addressing. I recommend placing your habits in the respective category of either "Anchor or Engine." This will aid in reducing the amount of confusion and increasing the effectiveness of your efforts. I saved the final chapter to discuss "Habits", reason being they are the keystones that fuse life together. Developing habits around happiness, forgiveness, innovation, exposure, education and execution augment the quality of life. These habits streamline decision-making, creating more time for beautiful and creative aspects of life. Know your purpose and grow your purpose by building a process that you can grow and learn to trust. Remaining clear on what it is we want out of life is vital, during our process of mental transformation. Whatever the challenge or adversity you're facing know that this is an opportunity for growth.

REINVENT YOURSELF

Through the steps mentioned throughout the book I was able to create the proper mindset and environment to tackle such adversity. I invite you to feel free to implement the techniques and adjust them to your satisfaction. I believe the best things come from most challenging times, where we are pushed and tested out of our comfort zone. Let the only competitor be the person in the mirror and strive to be the best version of you possible. Until we meet again let us remain strong, believe in ourselves and never give-up!

Made in the USA
Middletown, DE
21 February 2017